Spanish
Shortcut

By
Irineu De Oliveira Jnr

Copyright © 2013 Irineu De Oliveira Jnr.
All rights reserved.
ISBN-13: 978-1494328085
ISBN-10: 1494328089

TABLE OF CONTENTS

The History of the Spanish Language   6

CHAPTER 1. Phonetic Spanish Alphabet   7

CHAPTER 2. The Linguistic Secret   8

CHAPTER 3. -AL   12

CHAPTER 4. -SIÓN   14

CHAPTER 5. -DAD   15

CHAPTER 6. -DOR   18

CHAPTER 7. -ISTA   20

CHAPTER 8. -ICO or -ICA   23

CHAPTER 9. -ANTE   25

CHAPTER 10. -ENTE   27

CHAPTER 11. -AR VERBS   29

CHAPTER 12. -ARIO   32

CHAPTER 13. -MENTO   34

CHAPTER 14. -ENCIA   36

CHAPTER 15. -BLE   39

CHAPTER 16. -IVO   41

CHAPTER 17. -FICAR   44

CHAPTER 18. -GÍA   46

CHAPTER 19. -ORIO 49

CHAPTER 20. -IDO 51

CHAPTER 21. -IZAR 53

CHAPTER 22. -ANCIA 55

CHAPTER 23. -OSO 57

CHAPTER 24. -SIS 60

CHAPTER 25. -ISMO 63

CHAPTER 26. -AJE 66

CHAPTER 27. -AMA 68

CHAPTER 28. -EMA 70

CHAPTER 29. -IO 72

CHAPTER 30. -URA 74

CHAPTER 31. -TUD 76

CHAPTER 32. -ADA 78

CHAPTER 33. -CIA 80

CHAPTER 34. -FIA 83

CHAPTER 35. -ESO 85

CHAPTER 36. -OGO 86

CHAPTER 37. -EA 87

CHAPTER 38. -CULO 88

CHAPTER 39. -ANO 90

CHAPTER 40. -IA	92
CHAPTER 41. -PLO or -PLIO	93
CHAPTER 42. -INA	94
CHAPTER 43. -ENO	96
CHAPTER 44. -AR WORDS	98
CHAPTER 45. -METRO/-RO	100
CHAPTER 46. -OR	103
CHAPTER 47. VERB SHORTCUT	105

The History of the Spanish Language

The Spanish Language is a Romance language, i.e., it comes from the vulgar Latin language. More than 400 million people speak Spanish in the world today and Spanish is now definitely a language that everyone should learn.

Spanish has the status of the 4th most spoken language in the world. Spanish is spoken in 21 countries as the official language. From Latin America, to a large contingent in the United States, Spanish is growing in prominence. Present in former Spanish colonies such as the Philippines (Asia), Equatorial Guinea and the Western Sahara (Africa); the Spanish language also has great future projections for those who are interested in learning it, because of the wide socio-cultural repertoire offered. In 2050, the world is estimated to have over 530 million Spanish speakers, of which 100 million will be living in the United States. So if you want to survive in this globalized world, fluency in Spanish is important.

Its closest language is Galician, spoken in Galicia, located in north western Spain and north of Portugal. Spanish is very close to Portuguese too, which allows speakers of both languages to understand each other sometimes, but in many times there is misunderstanding and embarrassment.

In 1986, Spanish became one of the official languages of the European Union (EU) when Spain was admitted to the organization.

CHAPTER 1.
Phonetic Spanish Alphabet

Here is the alphabet phonetically written to allow you to compare the pronunciation of the English alphabet with the Spanish alphabet.

So concentrate on practicing the pronunciation of those letters which are not familiar to you.

A (ah), **B** (Bay), **C** (say), **Ch** (chay), **D** (day)

E (aay), **F** (effay), **G** (hay), **H** (ahchay), **I** (eee)

J (hotah), **K** (cah), **L** (ellay), **Ll** (ayyay), **M** (emmay)

N (ennay), **Ñ** (enyay), **O** (oh), P (pay), **Q** (coo)

R (airray), RR (airrrray), **S** (essay), T (tay), **U** (oooh)

V (bay), **W** (doughblay bay), **X** (aykeese)

Y (eee greeaygah), **Z** (saytah).

Spanish Shortcut

CHAPTER 2.
The Linguistic Secret

The linguistic secret is a conversion technique to create Spanish Words out of English.

For example, words ending in **TION** in English become **CIÓN** in Spanish.

English	**ESPAÑOL**
Informa**tion**	Informa**ción**

Translate these words into Spanish and then check the answers on the next page.

1. accusation _____
2. action _____
3. addition _____
4. affiliation _____
5. celebration _____
6. collection _____
7. creation _____
8. fiction _____
9. imperfection _____
10. introduction _____
11. lotion _____
12. simulation _____

Spanish Shortcut

Here are the Spanish words. Check if you got them right. You will also find many more words that you didn't know that you knew.

abreviación	coalición	creación
acción	cognición	cuestión
acreditación	colaboración	declaración
activación	colección	decoración
acusación	colonización	definición
adición	compensación	demolición
administración	complicación	demostración
admiración	comprobación	deportación
adopción	comunicación	descripción
adulación	concentración	desnutrición
afiliación	concepción	destrucción
aflicción	condición	detención
agitación	confederación	devastación
ambición	confirmación	diferenciación
animación	congregación	dirección
anotación	conservación	discreción
anticipación	consideración	discriminación
aplicación	consolación	disertación
apreciación	consolidación	distinción
aproximación	constipación	distracción
asimilación	construcción	distribución
atención	contaminación	diversificación
atenuación	contemplación	documentación
atracción	contracción	dominación
audición	contradicción	dramatización
autorización	contribución	edición
aviación	convención	educación
capacitación	convicción	elección
capitalización	cooperación	electrocución
celebración	coordinación	elevación
centralización	corporación	eliminación
circulación	corrección	emancipación
civilización	correlación	emigración
clasificación	corrupción	emoción

Spanish Shortcut

emulación	imaginación	liberación
erección	imitación	limitación
erupción	imperfección	loción
especialización	improvisación	lubricación
especificación	inauguración	manifestación
especulación	incitación	manipulación
estabilización	incorporación	meditación
esterilización	indiscreción	memorización
evaluación	infección	menstruación
evaporación	inflación	migración
evolución	inflamación	moderación
excavación	información	modificación
excepción	inhibición	monopolización
exclamación	innovación	motivación
expedición	inquisición	multiplicación
exploración	inspección	nación
exposición	inspiración	narración
extinción	instalación	negociación
extracción	institución	noción
falsificación	instrucción	nominación
federación	integración	nutrición
fermentación	intención	objeción
fertilización	interceptación	obligación
ficción	interdicción	observación
filtración	interrupción	obstrucción
fluctuación	intersección	ocupación
formulación	intervención	opción
fracción	intimidación	operación
fricción	introducción	oposición
fumigación	intuición	organización
función	invención	participación
fundación	invitación	percepción
generalización	irrigación	perfección
graduación	irritación	persecución
gravitación	justificación	personalización
identificación	legalización	poción
ilustración	legislación	polución

precaución
predicción
premonición
preposición
prescripción
presunción
prevención
privatización
proclamación
producción
promoción
pronunciación
proposición
prostitución
protección
provocación
publicación
puntuación
purificación
reacción
recepción
recomendación

reconciliación
recreación
recuperación
reducción
reelección
reencarnación
refrigeración
regulación
rehabilitación
renovación
reorganización
repetición
representación
reputación
resolución
respiración
revelación
revolución
rotación
satisfacción
saturación
sección

sedación
seducción
segregación
selección
separación
simplificación
simulación
situación
sofisticación
solución
superstición
tradición
transacción
transformación
transición
validación
variación
vegetación
ventilación
vibración
visualización

CHAPTER 3.
-AL

Most English words that end in **AL** are exactly like the Spanish ones with a few small spelling changes.

Here are the Spanish words.

abdominal	diagonal	fundamental
accidental	dictatorial	generacional
antisocial	diferencial	gramatical
anual	disfuncional	gravitacional
artificial	editorial	gutural
audio-visual	electoral	habitual
brutal	emocional	heterosexual
caníbal	esencial	homosexual
catedral	especial	horizontal
central	espinal	hormonal
cereal	espiritual	hospital
cerebral	estructural	ideal
ceremonial	excepcional	ilegal
colonial	existencial	imparcial
colosal	experimental	imperial
comercial	exponencial	impersonal
conceptual	factual	inaugural
condicional	fatal	individual
confidencial	federal	industrial
constitucional	fenomenal	infernal
continental	festival	informal
contractual	fetal	inicial
convencional	feudal	inmaterial
corporal	final	inmoral
correccional	fiscal	inmortal
criminal	floral	institucional
cristal	focal	instrumental
crucial	formal	integral
cultural	fraternal	intelectual
decimal	frugal	intencional
departamental	funcional	intercontinental

Spanish Shortcut

internacional
interracial
intestinal
irracional
jovial
lateral
liberal
literal
local
manual
marcial
marginal
marital
material
maternal
matriarcal
medieval
menstrual
mental
metal
mineral
modal
monumental
moral
mortal
multicultural
multifuncional
multinacional
mundial
municipal
mural
musical
nacional
nasal
natural
naval
neanderthal
nominal
normal
nutricional
ocasional
octagonal

ocupacional
oficial
operacional
oral
ordinal
original
ornamental
oval
papal
paranormal
parcial
parroquial
pastoral
patrimonial
pectoral
pedal
pedestal
penal
personal
plural
postal
potencial
preferencial
prenatal
presidencial
primordial
principal
profesional
proporcional
proverbial
provincial
puntual
racial
racional
radial
radical
real
recital
regional
residencial
residual
reverencial

ritual
rival
rural
secuencial
semifinal
sensacional
sensual
sentimental
sexual
sobrenatural
social
subliminal
subtropical
superficial
sustancial
terminal
territorial
tonal
torrencial
total
tradicional
transexual
transcendental
tribal
tropical
unilateral
universal
usual
verbal
vertical
viral
virtual
visual
vital
vocal

CHAPTER 4.
-SIÓN

Most English words that end in **SIÓN** are exactly like the Spanish ones with a few small spelling changes.

Here are the Spanish words.

abrasión	exclusión	persuasión
admisión	excursión	precisión
agresión	expansión	procesión
aprensión	explosión	profesión
aversión	expresión	progresión
colisión	expulsión	propulsión
comisión	extensión	radiodifusión
compasión	ilusión	recesión
comprensión	impresión	regresión
compresión	inclusión	remisión
concesión	indecisión	repercusión
conclusión	infusión	represión
confesión	inmersión	repulsión
confusión	intrusión	revisión
conversión	invasión	sesión
corrosión	inversión	supresión
decisión	misión	suspensión
depresión	obsesión	televisión
descompresión	ocasión	tensión
dimensión	omisión	transfusión
división	opresión	transmisión
emisión	pasión	versión
emulsión	pensión	visión
erosión	percusión	

Spanish Shortcut

CHAPTER 5.
-DAD

Words ending in **TY** in English become **DAD** in Spanish.

Translate these words into Spanish and then check the answers on the next page.

1. anxiety   _____
2. authority   _____
3. community   _____
4. identity   _____
5. mentality   _____
6. morality   _____
7. necessity   _____
8. obesity   _____
9. opportunity   _____
10. quantity   _____
11. reality   _____
12. responsibility _____

Spanish Shortcut

Here are the Spanish words. Check if you got them right. You will also find many more words that you didn't know that you knew.

accesibilidad	densidad	fragilidad
actividad	deshonestidad	fraternidad
adaptabilidad	dificultad	frugalidad
adversidad	dignidad	funcionalidad
afinidad	disparidad	generalidad
agilidad	diversidad	generosidad
ambigüedad	divinidad	hilaridad
amenidad	dualidad	hiperactividad
animosidad	duplicidad	homosexualidad
anormalidad	durabilidad	honestidad
ansiedad	elasticidad	hospitalidad
anualidad	electricidad	hostilidad
aplicabilidad	elegibilidad	humanidad
atrocidad	entidad	humedad
autenticidad	equidad	humildad
autoridad	especialidad	identidad
banalidad	espiritualidad	igualdad
brevedad	espontaneidad	ilegalidad
brutalidad	estabilidad	ilegibilidad
calamidad	esterilidad	imparcialidad
calidad	eternidad	imposibilidad
cantidad	eventualidad	improbabilidad
capacidad	exclusividad	impunidad
caridad	factibilidad	incapacidad
celebridad	falibilidad	incompatibilidad
ciudad	familiaridad	indignidad
civilidad	fatalidad	individualidad
compatibilidad	feminidad	inevitabilidad
comunidad	ferocidad	infalibilidad
continuidad	fertilidad	inferioridad
creatividad	fidelidad	infidelidad
credibilidad	finalidad	inflexibilidad
crueldad	flexibilidad	informalidad
curiosidad	formalidad	inmensidad

inmortalidad
inmunidad
inseguridad
integridad
intensidad
invisibilidad
invulnerabilidad
irracionalidad
irregularidad
irresponsabilidad
lealtad
legalidad
legibilidad
libertad
longevidad
magnanimidad
maleabilidad
marginalidad
masculinidad
maternidad
mediocridad
mentalidad
modalidad
modernidad
monstruosidad
moralidad
mortalidad
municipalidad
necesidad
negatividad
neutralidad

normalidad
novedad
obesidad
obscenidad
originalidad
oscuridad
oportunidad
paridad
particularidad
paternidad
perpetuidad
personalidad
perversidad
pluralidad
polaridad
popularidad
posibilidad
posteridad
prioridad
probabilidad
productividad
promiscuidad
propiedad
prosperidad
proximidad
publicidad
puntualidad
racionalidad
realidad
regularidad
relatividad

respetabilidad
responsabilidad
senilidad
sensibilidad
sensualidad
serenidad
sexualidad
simplicidad
sinceridad
singularidad
sobriedad
sociedad
solidaridad
subjetividad
superioridad
tenacidad
totalidad
trinidad
unidad
uniformidad
universidad
vanidad
variedad
versatilidad
virginidad
virilidad
viscosidad
visibilidad
vitalidad

CHAPTER 6.
-DOR

Words ending **TOR** in English become **DOR** in Spanish.

Translate these words into Spanish and then check the answers on the next page.

1. administrator   _____
2. aviator   _____
3. collaborator   _____
4. commentator   _____
5. communicator   _____
6. competitor   _____
7. coordinator   _____
8. creator   _____
9. decorator   _____
10. dictator   _____
11. distributor   _____
12. educator   _____

Spanish Shortcut

Here are the Spanish words. Check if you got them right. You will also find many more words that you didn't know that you knew.

administrador	dictador	instigador
aplicador	distribuidor	legislador
aviador	educador	mediador
comentador	exterminador	moderador
competidor	facilitador	narrador
comunicador	gladiador	operador
contribuidor	ilustrador	senador
coordinador	imitador	traidor
creador	indicador	violador
decorador	innovador	

CHAPTER 7.
-ISTA

Words ending in **IST** in English become **ISTA** in Spanish.

Translate these words into Spanish and then check the answers on the next page.

1. Baptist   _____
2. communist   _____
3. cyclist   _____
4. dentist   _____
5. extremist   _____
6. linguist   _____
7. list   _____
8. receptionist   _____
9. socialist   _____
10. specialist   _____
11. stylist   _____
12. tourist   _____

Spanish Shortcut

Here are the Spanish words. Check if you got them right. You will also find many more words that you didn't know that you knew.

absolutista	cabalista	dialoguista
activista	camorrista	diarista
alarmista	canonista	difusionista
alegorista	capitalista	dinamista
alpinista	caricaturista	documentalista
alquimista	catequista	ecologista
altruista	centralista	economista
ambientalista	centrista	ecoturista
analista	ceramista	educacionista
analogista	ciclista	egotista
anarquista	clarinetista	elitista
anatomista	clasicista	enciclopedista
anestesista	colaboracionista	epigrafista
anexionista	colectivista	equilibrista
animalista	colonialista	especialista
animista	colorista	estilista
antagonista	columnista	etimologista
arpista	comparatista	evangelista
artista	comunista	evolucionista
atomista	conservacionista	exorcista
autista	constitucionalista	extremista
automatista	constructivista	fascista
automovilista	consumista	feminista
autonomista	contorsionista	finalista
balista	contrabandista	flautista
bautista	cooperativista	florista
bimetalista	corporativista	folclorista
budista	dentista	genealogista
generalista	iluminista	instrumentista
guitarrista	ilusionista	integracionista
hiperrealista	imperialista	intelectualista
humanista	individualista	internacionalista
humorista	inflacionista	intervencionista
idealista	institucionalista	irracionalista

legista
lingüista
lista
liturgista
localista
logista
luminista
manierista
maquinista
masoquista
materialista
maximalista
medallista
metodista
militarista
modelista
modernista
monetarista
moralista
motociclista
nacionalista
narcisista
nativista
naturalista

nepotista
nudista
nutricionista
objetivista
oculista
ocultista
oportunista
oposicionista
optimista
optometrista
organista
orientalista
ortodontista
ortopedista
pacifista
parodista
percusionista
perfeccionista
personalista
pesimista
pianista
pluralista
polemista
populista

positivista
pragmatista
progresista
propagandista
protagonista
proteccionista
proyectista
publicista
racionalista
racista
realista
recepcionista
reformista
relativista
salmista
saxofonista
sexista
socialista
solista
terrorista
trapecista
turista
violinista

Spanish Shortcut

CHAPTER 8.
-ICO or -ICA

Words ending in **IC** or **ICAL** in English become **ICO** or **ICA** in Spanish.

Translate these words into Spanish and then check the answers on the next page.

1. acoustic　　　_____
2. antiseptic　　_____
3. Catholic　　　_____
4. diabetic　　　_____
5. economical　　_____
6. magical　　　_____
7. mathematical　_____
8. mechanic　　　_____
9. philosophical　_____
10. poetical　　　_____
11. political　　　_____
12. technical　　　_____

Spanish Shortcut

Here are the Spanish words. Check if you got them right. You will also find many more words that you didn't know that you knew.

alérgico	ecológico	mecánico
alfabético	económico	metafísico
analítico	eléctrico	metafórico
acústico	empírico	metódico
anémico	epiléptico	místico
anestésico	escéptico	mítico
anoréxico	esférico	mitológico
antibiótico	estadístico	neurológico
antiséptico	ética	numérico
arqueológico	evangélico	óptico
astrológico	fanático	ortopédico
astronómico	farmacéutico	pediátrico
autobiográfico	filosófico	poético
bíblico	gástrico	político
biográfico	genealógico	práctico
biológico	geográfico	psicológico
botánico	geológico	psiquiátrico
católico	geométrico	retórica
cíclico	geriátrico	sabático
cilíndrico	hipodérmico	satírico
cínico	hipotético	simétrico
clásico	histérico	sintomático
clínico	histórico	táctico
cólico	holístico	técnico
cómico	idéntico	tecnológico
crítico	ideológico	teológico
crónico	ilógico	terapéutico
cúbico	irónico	típico
demográfico	lírica	tónico
diabético	lógica	tóxico
diabólico	logística	traumático
disléxico	mágico	
eclesiástico	matemático	

CHAPTER 9.
-ANTE

Words ending in **ANT** in English become **ANTE** in Spanish.

Translate these words into Spanish and then check the answers on the next page.

1. abundant _____
2. brillant _____
3. commandant _____
4. constant _____
5. deodorant _____
6. distant _____
7. elephant _____
8. giant _____
9. immigrant _____
10. important _____
11. intolerant _____
12. restaurant _____

Spanish Shortcut

Here are the Spanish words. Check if you got them right. You will also find many more words that you didn't know that you knew.

abundante		participante
ambulante	gigante	penetrante
antioxidante	habitante	persevante
arrogante	hidrante	picante
brillante	ignorante	precipitante
cohabitante	implante	predominante
colorante	importante	preponderante
comandante	incesante	protestante
comerciante	infante	pulsante
concursante	informante	quadrante
consonante	inmigrante	radiante
constante	insignificante	recombinante
contaminante	instante	redundante
culminante	intolerante	registrante
debutante	intrigante	reimplante
declarante	irrelevante	relevante
desinfectante	irritante	resonante
desodorante	manifestante	restaurante
distante	mercante	resultante
dominante	migrante	solicitante
elefante	militante	suplicante
elegante	mutante	tolerante
emigrante	negociante	trasplante
excitante	observante	triunfante
exorbitante	ocupante	vibrante
expectante	oficiante	vacante
extravagante	otorgante	
fulminante	oxidante	

CHAPTER 10.
-ENTE

Words ending in **ENT** in English become **ENTE** in Spanish.

Translate these words into Spanish and then check the answers on the next page.

1. accident   _____
2. agent   _____
3. client   _____
4. competent   _____
5. continent   _____
6. different   _____
7. diligent   _____
8. excellent   _____
9. innocent   _____
10. permanent   _____
11. president   _____
12. urgent   _____

Spanish Shortcut

Here are the Spanish words. Check if you got them right. You will also find many more words that you didn't know that you knew.

accidente	elocuente	insolente
adyacente	eminente	inteligente
adolescente	equivalente	intermitente
agente	evidente	latente
ambivalente	excelente	negligente
antecedente	fluorescente	omnipresente
aparente	frecuente	omnisciente
cliente	impaciente	paciente
coherente	impertinente	permanente
competente	imprudente	pertinente
continente	incandescente	presidente
contingente	incidente	reciente
convergente	incompetente	residente
decadente	inconsecuente	reticente
decente	indecente	serpiente
detergente	indiferente	torrente
diferente	indulgente	transparente
diligente	ingrediente	urgente
disidente	inherente	vehemente
divergente	inocente	vicepresidente

Spanish Shortcut

CHAPTER 11.
-AR VERBS

Words ending in **ATE** in English become **AR** in Spanish.

Translate these words into Spanish and then check the answers on the next page.

1. administrate _____
2. calculate _____
3. celebrate _____
4. communicate _____
5. decorate _____
6. donate _____
7. educate _____
8. graduate _____
9. investigate _____
10. participate _____
11. separate _____
12. terminate _____

Spanish Shortcut

Here are the Spanish words. Check if you got them right. You will also find many more words that you didn't know that you knew.

abreviar	contemplar	enumerar
acelerar	cooperar	enunciar
acumular	coordinar	equivocar
administrar	corroborar	especular
afiliar	crear	estimar
agitar	cultivar	estrangular
agravar	debilitar	evaporar
alegar	decapitar	exagerar
alienar	decorar	exasperar
amputar	degenerar	excavar
animar	delegar	exfoliar
anticipar	denigrar	exterminar
apreciar	denunciar	fabricar
articular	depreciar	facilitar
asesinar	designar	fascinar
asfixiar	deteriorar	felicitar
asimilar	devastar	filtrar
asociar	diferenciar	formular
autenticar	dilatar	fornicar
calcular	disculpar	frustrar
castigar	diseminar	fumigar
castrar	dislocar	graduar
celebrar	domesticar	generar
circular	dominar	gesticular
coagular	donar	gofrar
compensar	duplicar	habituar
complicar	educar	hesitar
comunicar	elaborar	humillar
condensar	eliminar	imitar
confiscar	emanar	implicar
conjugar	emancipar	inaugurar
consagrar	emigrar	incinerar
consolidar	enfocar	incriminar
contaminar	entrar	incubar

Spanish Shortcut

indicar	motivar	regurgitar
infiltrar	mutilar	rehabilitar
iniciar	navegar	relegar
inmigrar	necesitar	remunerar
inocular	negociar	renovar
insinuar	nombrar	repatriar
integrar	orquestar	revalidar
interrogar	oxigenar	rotar
intimidar	palpar	saturar
intoxicar	participar	separar
investigar	perforar	sincopar
irradiar	perpetuar	situar
irrigar	predominar	subordinar
irritar	premeditar	suscitar
lacerar	proliferar	tolerar
liberar	propagar	trazar
liquidar	reanimar	terminar
lubricar	recontar	ventilar
manejar	recuperar	validar
manipular	refrigerar	vegetar
masticar	regenerar	
meditar	regular	

Spanish Shortcut

CHAPTER 12.
-ARIO

Words ending in **ARY** in English become **ARIO** in Spanish.

Translate these words into Spanish and then check the answers on the next page.

1. adversary _____
2. anniversary _____
3. dictionary _____
4. glossary _____
5. intermediary _____
6. legendary _____
7. necessary _____
8. salary _____
9. secretary _____
10. temporary _____
11. visionary _____
12. vocabulary _____

Spanish Shortcut

Here are the Spanish words. Check if you got them right. You will also find many more words that you didn't know that you knew.

adversario	honorario	revolucionario
aniversario	imaginario	rudimentario
arbitrario	intermediario	salario
binario	involuntario	sanitario
complementario	legendario	santuario
contrario	literario	secretario
coronario	mercenario	secundario
culinario	monetario	sedimentario
diccionario	necesario	solitario
dignatario	notario	temporario
disciplinario	ordinario	terciario
dispensario	ovario	ternario
estacionario	penitenciario	veterinario
extraordinario	planetario	visionario
glosario	primario	vocabulario
hereditario	reaccionario	voluntario

Spanish Shortcut

CHAPTER 13.
-MENTO

Words ending in **MENT** in English become **MENTO** in Spanish.

Translate these words into Spanish and then check the answers on the next page.

1. apartment   _____

2. document   _____

3. element   _____

4. instrument   _____

5. monument   _____

6. movement   _____

7. parliament   _____

8. supplement   _____

9. testament   _____

10. torment   _____

Spanish Shortcut

Here are the Spanish words. Check if you got them right. You will also find many more words that you didn't know that you knew.

alimento	fermento	parlamento
apartamento	filamento	pigmento
aplazamiento	firmamento	reglamento
argumento	fragmento	reprocesamiento
armamento	fundamento	rudimento
cemento	incremento	sacramento
compartimiento	instrumento	segmento
complemento	ligamento	suplemento
comportamiento	medicamento	temperamento
condimento	monumento	testamento
decremento	movimiento	tormento
documento	multifilamento	
elemento	ornamento	

Spanish Shortcut

CHAPTER 14.
-ENCIA

Words ending in **ENCE** in English become **ENCIA** in Spanish.

Translate these words into Spanish and then check the answers on the next page.

1. adolescence _____
2. circumference _____
3. coincidence _____
4. conference _____
5. correspondence _____
6. difference _____
7. evidence _____
8. experience _____
9. influence _____
10. preference _____
11. presence _____
12. science _____

Spanish Shortcut

Here are the Spanish words. Check if you got them right. You will also find many more words that you didn't know that you knew.

ausencia	corpulencia	existencia
abstinencia	influencia	experiencia
adherencia	violencia	feculencia
adolescencia	covalencia	flatulencia
ambivalencia	decadencia	florencia
antecedencia	dehiscencia	fluorescencia
bioluminiscencia	delicuescencia	frecuencia
birrefringencia	detumescencia	inmanencia
cadencia	diferencia	inminencia
ciencia	diligencia	impaciencia
circunferencia	disidencia	impenitencia
coexistencia	divergencia	impermanencia
correspondencia	efervescencia	impertinencia
coincidencia	eflorescencia	imprudencia
competencia	efluencia	impudencia
concrescencia	elocuencia	incidencia
concupiscencia	apariencia	incipiencia
conferencia	eminencia	incoherencia
confluencia	equipolencia	incompetencia
congruencia	equivalencia	incongruencia
conciencia	esencia	inconsecuencia
consecuencia	etnociencia	incontinencia
continencia	evanescencia	indiferencia
contingencia	evidencia	indigencia
convalecencia	excelencia	indolencia
convergencia	exigencia	indulgencia

inexistencia	opulencia	residencia
inexperiencia	paciencia	renuencia
inferencia	penitencia	ciencia
infrecuencia	permanencia	secuencia
inherencia	pertinencia	soñolencia
inocencia	fosforescencia	estridencia
insolencia	potencia	subsistencia
inteligencia	preeminencia	suculencia
interferencia	preexistencia	supe inteligencia
inter-influencia	preferencia	tangencia
irreverencia	presciencia	teleconferencia
jurisprudencia	presencia	tendencia
licencia	providencia	transparencia
luminiscencia	prudencia	tumescencia
magnificencia	pseudociencia	turbulencia
munificencia	pubescencia	turgencia
negligencia	purulencia	valencia
obsolescencia	quintaesencia	videoconferencia
ocurrencia	recurrencia	virulencia
omnipresencia	reemergencia	
omnisciencia	referencia	
opalescencia	reminiscencia	

CHAPTER 15.
-BLE

Most English words that end in **BLE** are exactly like the Spanish ones with a few small spelling changes.

Here are the Spanish words.

aceptable	demostrable	improbable
adaptable	deplorable	inaccesible
admirable	determinable	inaceptable
admisible	detestable	inadmisible
adorable	divisible	inalienable
ajustable	excitable	inaudible
apreciable	explicable	incalculable
audible	explotable	incomparable
biodegradable	exportable	incomprensible
calculable	falible	inconsolable
combustible	favorable	incontrolable
comparable	flexible	incorruptible
compatible	formidable	incurable
considerable	habitable	indefinible
consolable	honorable	indescriptible
consumible	horrible	indiscutible
controlable	ilegible	indispensable
convertible	imaginable	indistinguible
corruptible	impecable	inestimable
culpable	imposible	inevitable
cuestionable	impresionable	inexplicable

infalible	lamentable	programable
inflamable	legible	reparable
inflexible	maleable	respetable
inimaginable	memorable	responsable
ininteligible	negociable	reversible
inoperable	notable	separable
insaciable	observable	sociable
inseparable	operable	sostenible
insociable	palpable	tangible
intolerable	pasable	terrible
invariable	perdonable	tolerable
invisible	plausible	transferible
irreconciliable	posible	variable
irresistible	preferible	viable
irrevocable	presentable	visible
irritable	probable	vulnerable

Spanish Shortcut

CHAPTER 16.
-IVO

Words ending in **IVE** in English become **IVO** in Spanish.

Translate these words into Spanish and then check the answers on the next page.

1. active _____
2. administrative _____
3. aggressive _____
4. archive _____
5. creative _____
6. exclusive _____
7. executive _____
8. fugitive _____
9. intensive _____
10. negative _____
11. positive _____
12. productive _____

Spanish Shortcut

Here are the Spanish words. Check if you got them right. You will also find many more words that you didn't know that you knew.

ablativo
abortivo
abrasivo
abusivo
relativo
acumulativo
acusativo
activo
aditivo
adhesivo
adjetivo
administrativo
adoptivo
afectivo
agresivo
alusivo
antitusivo
apelativo
asociativo
archivo
atributivo
aumentativo
aversivo
bioactivo
capacitivo
cautivo
carminativo
coactivo
cognitivo
cohesivo
colectivo
conmemorativo
comunicativo
comparativo
compensativo
competitivo
completivo
compulsivo
concesivo

definitivo
conectivo
connotativo
consecutivo
constitutivo
constructivo
contemplativo
continuativo
anticonceptivo
convulsivo
copulativo
correctivo
correlativo
corroborativo
corrosivo
corruptivo
creativo
curativo
dativo
decisivo
declarativo
decorativo
deductivo
demostrativo
denominativo
depresivo
descriptivo
destructivo
difusivo
digestivo
diminutivo
discursivo
disyuntivo
dispersivo
disociativo
distintivo
distributivo
educativo
electivo

electronegativo
electropositivo
eliminativo
emisivo
erosivo
eruptivo
evaluativo
evasivo
excesivo
exclusivo
ejecutivo
expansivo
explicativo
explosivo
expresivo
extractivo
facultativo
federativo
figurativo
frecuentativo
fugitivo
generativo
genitivo
hiperactivo
ilativo
imaginativo
imitativo
imperativo
impulsivo
inactivo
incisivo
indicativo
inductivo
inexpresivo
infinitivo
informativo
inofensivo
instintivo
instructivo

intensivo
interactivo
interpretativo
interrogativo
intransitivo
introspectivo
intuitivo
inventivo
radiativo
legislativo
locativo
lucrativo
masivo
pensativo
motivo
multiplicativo
negativo
nominativo
normativo
nutritivo
objetivo
obstructivo
opresivo
optativo
oxidativo
paliativo
partitivo
pasivo
peyorativo
perceptivo
perfectivo
permisivo
persuasivo
positivo
posesivo
predicativo
preventivo
primitivo
productivo
progresivo
prohibitivo
prescriptivo
punitivo
putativo
cualitativo
cuantitativo
radioactivo
reactivo
receptivo
recesivo
recreativo
refractivo
regresivo
reiterativo
repetitivo
represivo
repulsivo
respectivo
restrictivo
retroactivo
sedativo
separativo
significativo
especulativo
deportivo
subjetivo
subjuntivo
sustantivo
subversivo
sucesivo
sugestivo
superlativo
suspensivo
transitivo
improductivo
vegetativo
vengativo
vocativo
votivo

Spanish Shortcut

CHAPTER 17.
-FICAR

Words ending in **IFY** in English become **IFICAR** in Spanish.

Translate these words into Spanish and then check the answers on the next page.

1. amplify _____
2. certify _____
3. classify _____
4. diversify _____
5. identify _____
6. intensify _____
7. justify _____
8. modify _____
9. qualify _____
10. specify _____
11. testify _____
12. verify _____

Spanish Shortcut

Here are the Spanish words. Check if you got them right. You will also find many more words that you didn't know that you knew.

acidificar	ejemplificar	purificar
amplificar	escarificar	ratificar
beatificar	especificar	recalificar
calcificar	estratificar	recertificar
calificar	falsificar	recodificar
certificar	fortificar	rectificar
codificar	fructificar	reunificar
clasificar	gasificar	revivificar
cosificar	glorificar	sacarificar
crucificar	humidificar	salificar
cuantificar	identificar	santificar
deificar	intensificar	saponificar
densificar	justificar	simplificar
desacidificar	mistificar	solidificar
descalificar	modificar	testificar
desclasificar	momificar	unificar
deshumidificar	mortificar	verificar
desmitificar	osificar	vitrificar
desnitrificar	pacificar	vivificar
diversificar	personificar	
edificar	petrificar	

CHAPTER 18.
-GÍA

Words ending in **GY** in English become **GÍA** in Spanish.

Translate these words into Spanish and then check the answers on the next page.

1. allergy　　　　_____
2. biology　　　　_____
3. ideology　　　 _____
4. morphology　　_____
5. mythology　　　_____
6. pedagogy　　　 _____
7. physiology　　　_____
8. psychology　　　_____
9. radiology　　　 _____
10. sociology　　　_____
11. technology　　 _____
12. theology　　　 _____

Spanish Shortcut

Here are the Spanish words. Check if you got them right. You will also find many more words that you didn't know that you knew.

alergia	mineralogía	organología
biología	miología	orgía
dermatología	misionología	ornitología
ecología	mistagogía	osteología
edafología	mitología	otología
enología	mixología	paleoantropología
espeleología	morfología	paleobiología
estereología	museología	paleoclimatología
estrategia	musicología	paleoecología
farmacología	narratología	paleontología
fenología	nefrología	paleozoología
fenomenología	nematología	palinología
ficología	neonatología	parasicología
filología	neurobiología	parasitología
fisiología	neurofisiología	patología
fisiopatología	neurología	pedagogía
fitopatología	neuropatología	petrología
flebología	neuropsicología	planetología
fonología	neurorradiología	pneumatología
fotobiología	nomología	polifagia
fotogeología	nosología	praxeología
fraseología	numerología	primatología
frenología	oceanología	proctología
ideología	oftalmología	protozoología
micología	oncología	psicobiología
microcirugía	ontología	psicofisiología

Spanish Shortcut

psicología	sinergia	terminología
psicopatología	sinología	tetralogía
radiobiología	sintomatología	tipología
radioecología	sismología	topología
radiología	sociobiología	toxicología
reflexología	sociología	tribología
reología	somatología	tricología
reumatología	soteriología	trilogía
sedimentología	tanatología	ufología
semasiología	taumaturgia	urología
serología	tautología	victimología
sexología	tecnología	virología
sicigia	teleología	vulcanología
simbología	tcología	zoología
sinecología	teratología	

Spanish Shortcut

CHAPTER 19.
-ORIO

Words ending in **ORY** in English become **ORIO** or **ORIA** in Spanish.

Translate these words into Spanish and then check the answers on the next page.

1. accessory   _____

2. conservatory   _____

3. discriminatory   _____

4. history   _____

5. laboratory   _____

6. observatory   _____

7. preparatory   _____

8. refectory   _____

9. territory   _____

Spanish Shortcut

Here are the Spanish words. Check if you got them right. You will also find many more words that you didn't know that you knew.

accesorio	ilusorio	preparatorio
anti-inflamatorio	inflamatorio	promontorio
compensatorio	interlocutorio	purgatorio
conservatorio	conservatorio	refectorio
contradictorio	laboratorio	repertorio
difamatorio	migratorio	respiratorio
discriminatorio	obligatorio	supositorio
exploratorio	observatorio	territorio
historia	perentorio	

Spanish Shortcut

CHAPTER 20.
-IDO

Words ending in **ID** in English become **IDO** in Spanish.

Translate these words into Spanish and then check the answers on the next page.

1. acid   _____
2. fluid   _____
3. hybrid   _____
4. invalid _____
5. liquid   _____
6. timid   _____
7. stupid   _____
8. solid   _____
9. rapid   _____
10. rigid   _____
11. humid   _____

Spanish Shortcut

Here are the Spanish words. Check if you got them right. You will also find many more words that you didn't know that you knew.

ácido	fásmido	líquido
actínido	fluido	lívido
anélido	frígido	lúcido
antiácido	híbrido	monoácido
arácnido	hidrácido	mórbido
aramida	húmedo	rápido
árido	ilíquido	rígido
ávido	insípido	sólido
cándido	inválido	tímido
dióxido	límpido	
estúpido	lípido	

Spanish Shortcut

CHAPTER 21.
-IZAR

Words ending in **IZE** in English become **IZAR** in Spanish.

Translate these words into Spanish and then check the answers on the next page.

1. analyze _____
2. authorize _____
3. capitalize _____
4. colonize _____
5. commercialize _____
6. formalize _____
7. nationalize _____
8. organize _____
9. socialize _____
10. specialize _____
11. utilize _____
12. materialize _____

Spanish Shortcut

Here are the Spanish words. Check if you got them right. You will also find many more words that you didn't know that you knew.

actualizar	fraternizar	naturalizar
alcalinizar	galvanizar	neutralizar
almacenar	generalizar	normalizar
analizar	homogenizar	optimizar
armonizar	hospitalizar	organizar
atomizar	humanizar	paralizar
autorizar	idealizar	penalizar
bautizar	impermeabilizar	personalizar
capitalizar	improvisar	polarizar
caracterizar	individualizar	popularizar
carbonizar	industrializar	privatizar
centralizar	inmortalizar	profesionalizar
colectivizar	inmunizar	profetizar
colonizar	intelectualizar	satirizar
comercializar	interiorizar	secularizar
cristalizar	ionizar	simbolizar
democratizar	liberalizar	sincronizar
dogmatizar	localizar	singularizar
dramatizar	magnetizar	sintetizar
escandalizar	materializar	sistematizar
especializar	maximizar	socializar
espiritualizar	mecanizar	teorizar
estabilizar	militarizar	tiranizar
estandarizar	miniaturizar	traumatizar
esterilizar	minimizar	trivializar
evangelizar	modernizar	urbanizar
exorcizar	monetizar	utilizar
exteriorizar	monopolizar	vaporizar
familiarizar	moralizar	visualizar
fertilizar	motorizar	vocalizar
formalizar	movilizar	
fosilizar	nacionalizar	

CHAPTER 22.
-ANCIA

Words ending in **ANCE** in English become **ANCIA** in Spanish.

Translate these words into Spanish and then check the answers on the next page.

1. abundance _____

2. substance _____

3. tolerance _____

4. France _____

5. elegance _____

6. distance _____

7. ignorance _____

8. importance _____

Spanish Shortcut

Here are the Spanish words. Check if you got them right. You will also find many more words that you didn't know that you knew.

absorbancia	extravagancia	invariancia
abundancia	exuberancia	luminancia
ambulancia	flagrancia	penetrancia
arrogancia	Francia	perseverancia
asonancia	hipervigilancia	preponderancia
circunstancia	ignorancia	protuberancia
concordancia	impedancia	reactancia
conductancia	importancia	repugnancia
consonancia	inductancia	resonancia
disonancia	insignificancia	sustancia
distancia	intemperancia	tolerancia
elegancia	intolerancia	vigilancia

Spanish Shortcut

CHAPTER 23.
-OSO

Words ending in **OUS** in English become **OSO** in Spanish.

Translate these words into Spanish and then check the answers on the next page.

1. ambitious   _____
2. delicious   _____
3. fabulous   _____
4. furious   _____
5. industrious   _____
6. ingenious   _____
7. precious   _____
8. religious   _____
9. spacious   _____
10. studious   _____
11. vicious   _____
12. victorious   _____

Spanish Shortcut

Here are the Spanish words. Check them. If you got them right, you will find many more words that you didn't know that you knew.

aluminoso	delicioso	generoso
ambicioso	desastroso	giboso
amoroso	desventajoso	glorioso
angiomatoso	envidioso	glutinoso
ansioso	escabroso	grumoso
arcilloso	escandaloso	horroroso
arenoso	escrofuloso	ignominioso
armonioso	escrupuloso	impetuoso
arsenioso	espacioso	incestuoso
bilioso	especioso	incurioso
brumoso	esponjoso	industrioso
bulboso	eslertoroso	infeccioso
calamitoso	estudioso	ingenioso
canceroso	fabuloso	insidioso
capcioso	faccioso	laborioso
caprichoso	fastidioso	laminoso
cavernoso	ferroso	leproso
ceremonioso	ferruginoso	libidinoso
ceroso	fervoroso	licencioso
chistoso	fibroso	litigioso
compendioso	filamentoso	lujoso
condilomatoso	fosforoso	luminoso
contagioso	furioso	malicioso
copioso	gangrenoso	maravilloso
cromoso	gaseoso	melindroso
curioso	gelatinoso	melodioso

membranoso	piadoso	seroso
microporoso	piojoso	sinuoso
milagroso	pomposo	supersticioso
misterioso	poroso	tedioso
monstruoso	precioso	tendencioso
montañoso	pretencioso	tenebroso
mucilaginoso	prestigioso	tortuoso
mucinoso	presuntuoso	tumultuoso
mucoso	prodigioso	ventajoso
nebuloso	pulposo	verminoso
nervioso	quisquilloso	vertiginoso
nitroso	religioso	vicioso
numeroso	riguroso	victorioso
odioso	ruinoso	vinoso
oleorresinoso	sanioso	virtuoso
parsimonioso	sedicioso	viscoso
pernicioso	semiprecioso	voluminoso
petroso	sentencioso	

CHAPTER 24.
-SIS

Most English words that end in **SIS** are exactly like the Spanish ones with a few small spelling changes.

Here are the Spanish words.

aféresis	babesiosis	clorosis
alcalosis	bacteriostasis	coccidiosis
amaurosis	biocenosis	colestasis
amibiasis	biogénesis	criptoanálisis
amitosis	biosíntesis	crisis
amniocentesis	bisinosis	cyanogenesis
anagénesis	blastomicosis	dermatosis
análisis	brucelosis	diacinesis
anaplasmosis	calcinosis	diaforesis
anastomosis	candidiasis	diagénesis
angiogénesis	carcinogénesis	diálisis
anquilosis	carcinomatosis	diapedesis
antesis	catachresis	diartrosis
antibiosis	cataforesis	diátesis
antífrasis	catálisis	diuresis
antítesis	catequesis	diverticulosis
apódosis	cetogénesis	electroanálisis
apoptosis	cetosis	electrodiálisis
apoteosis	chromatolysis	electroforesis
arteriosclerosis	cianosis	electrogénesis
artrodesis	ciclogénesis	electrólisis
asbestosis	ciclosis	electroosmosis
ascariasis	cifosis	embriogénesis
aspergilosis	cirrosis	endocitosis
aterogénesis	cisticercosis	endometriosis
aterosclerosis	citocinesis	endomitosis
autocatálisis	citolisis	epenthesis
autolisis	cladogénesis	epífisis

60

Spanish Shortcut

epigénesis	gluconeogénesis	metempsicosis
epirogénesis	gnosis	miasis
equinococosis	helmintiasis	micosis
eritroblastosis	hematopoyesis	microanálisis
eritropoyesis	hemodiálisis	midriasis
esclerosis	hemólisis	mielofibrosis
escoliosis	heterólisis	mitosis
espermatogénesis	hidrólisis	mixomatosis
espiroquetosis	Hiperhidrosis	moniliasis
esporotricosis	hiperostosis	monogénesis
esquistosomiasis	hiperqueratosis	mononucleosis
estasis	hipervitaminosis	morfogénesis
estenosis	hipnosis	mutagénesis
esteroidogénesis	hipóstasis	narcosis
estrongiloidiasis	hipótesis	natriuresis
exégesis	histéresis	necrosis
exocitosis	histogénesis	nefrosis
exostosis	histólisis	neumoconiosis
fagocitosis	histoplasmosis	neurosis
fascioliasis	leishmaniasis	noesis
fibrinólisis	leptospirosis	nucleosíntesis
fibrosis	leucocitosis	oncocercosis
filariasis	leucopoyesis	oncogénesis
fluorosis	linfocitosis	organogénesis
fosforolisis	linfomatosis	ornitosis
fotólisis	lipólisis	orogénesis
fotosíntesis	lisis	ortesis
frontogénesis	listeriosis	ortogénesis
frontólisis	litiasis	ósmosis
furunculosis	lordosis	osteogénesis
gametogénesis	macrocitosis	osteoporosis
génesis	meiosis	otosclerosis
giardiasis	melanogénesis	ovogénesis
ginogénesis	meta-análisis	paedomorphosis
glicogénesis	metamorfosis	paréntesis
glucogenolisis	metástasis	partenogénesis
glucólisis	metátesis	pedogénesis

Spanish Shortcut

petrogénesis	radiolysis	teniasis
pinocitosis	reanálisis	tesis
pirolisis	resíntesis	tirotoxicosis
plasmaféresis	salmonelosis	toxicosis
poliedrosis	sarcoidosis	toxoplasmosis
polinosis	sarcomatosis	tricomoniasis
prótasis	siderosis	tripanosomiasis
proteólisis	silepsis	triquinosis
prótesis	silicosis	trombosis
Psicoanálisis	simbiosis	tuberculosis
psicogénesis	sindesmosis	tumorigénesis
psiconeurosis	sinéresis	urolitiasis
psicosíntesis	sínfisis	virosis
psicosis	sinostosis	vitelogénesis
psitacosis	síntesis	xerosis
quimiosíntesis	solvólisis	zoonosis

Spanish Shortcut

CHAPTER 25.
-ISMO

Words ending in **ISM** in English become **ISMO** in Spanish.

Translate these words into Spanish and then check the answers on the next page.

1. activism _____
2. alcoholism _____
3. athleticism _____
4. autism _____
5. capitalism _____
6. fanaticism _____
7. fascism _____
8. federalism _____
9. racism _____
10. socialism _____
11. terrorism _____
12. vandalism _____

Spanish Shortcut

Here are the Spanish words. Check them. If you got them right, you will find many more words that you didn't know that you knew.

abolicionismo
absentismo
absolutismo
academicismo
acromatismo
actinismo
activismo
adopcionismo
aforismo
agrarismo
alarmismo
albinismo
alcoholismo
alelismo
altruismo
anabaptismo
anabolismo
anacronismo
analfabetismo
anarquismo
anglicismo
animalismo
animismo
antagonismo
anticomunismo
antirrealismo
arribismo
ascetismo
asociacionismo
asterismo
astigmatismo
atavismo
atletismo
atomismo

autismo
autoerotismo
automorfismo
autoritarismo
aventurerismo
baalismo
biblicismo
bicameralismo
biculturalismo
bilateralismo
bilingüismo
bimetalismo
biologismo
biorregionalismo
bipartidismo
bolchevismo
botulismo
bruxismo
burocratismo
caciquismo
canibalismo
capitalismo
catabolismo
catastrofismo
catecismo
centralismo
centrismo
chauvinismo
cinconismo
cinismo
clasicismo
clasismo
clericalismo
colectivismo

colonialismo
colorismo
comensalismo
comunalismo
comunismo
conceptualismo
concretismo
confesionalismo
conformismo
conservatismo
constructivismo
consumismo
convencionalismo
corporalivismo
cosmopolitanismo
creacionismo
cretinismo
cromatismo
cultismo
curanderismo
demonismo
derrotismo
despotismo
determinismo
diamagnetismo
diastrofismo
dicromatismo
difusionismo
diletantismo
dimorfismo
dinamismo
divisionismo
doctrinarismo
dogmatismo

druidismo
dualismo
eclecticismo
ecoterrorismo
ecoturismo
ecumenismo
egocentrismo
egotismo
elitismo
empirismo
enanismo
enciclopedismo
endemismo
epigonismo
eremitismo
eretismo
ergotismo
erotismo
esencialismo

esoterismo
estatismo
esteticismo
etnocentrismo
eudemonismo
eufemismo
eufuismo
evemerismo
evolucionismo
excepcionalismo
exclusivismo
exhibicionismo
existencialismo
exorcismo
expansionismo
experimentalismo
expresionismo
externalismo

extremismo
faccionalismo
familismo
fanatismo
fascismo
fatalismo
fauvismo
favoritismo
federalismo
igualitarismo
mercantilismo
montañismo
quimerismo
quimiotropismo
racismo
socialismo
terrorismo
vandalismo

Spanish Shortcut

CHAPTER 26.
-AJE

Words ending in **AGE** in English become **AJE** in Spanish.

Translate these words into Spanish and then check the answers on the next page.

1. courage   _____

2. drainage   _____

3. garage   _____

4. homage   _____

5. massage   _____

6. message   _____

7. passage   _____

8. reportage   _____

9. sabotage   _____

10. voltage   _____

66

Spanish Shortcut

Here are the Spanish words. Check them. If you got them right, you will find many more words that you didn't know that you knew.

agiotaje	ensilaje	masaje
amperaje	equipaje	mensaje
anclaje	espionaje	metalenguaje
arbitraje	factoraje	metraje
bagaje	forraje	montaje
blindaje	fotomontaje	pasaje
boscaje	fuselaje	pelaje
cabotaje	garaje	pillaje
camionaje	herbaje	reportaje
camuflaje	homenaje	sabotaje
chantaje	kilometraje	salvaje
coraje	libertinaje	señoreaje
corretaje	linaje	voltaje
drenaje	masaje	

Spanish Shortcut

CHAPTER 27.
-AMA

Words ending in **AM** in English become **AMA** or **AMO** in Spanish.

Translate these words into Spanish and then check the answers on the next page.

1. aerogram　　　　　_____

2. cardiogram　　　　_____

3. diagram　　　　　 _____

4. program　　　　　_____

5. telegram　　　　　_____

6. electrocardiogram　_____

7. hologram　　　　　_____

8. hexagram　　　　　_____

9. photogram　　　　 _____

Spanish Shortcut

Here are the Spanish words. Check them. If you got them right, you will find many more words that you didn't know that you knew.

aerograma	ecocardiograma	histograma
amalgama	ecograma	holograma
anagrama	electrocardiograma	ideograma
audiograma	electroferograma	logograma
barograma	electrograma	miligramo
cablegrama	electromiograma	monograma
caprolactama	engrama	pictograma
cardiograma	epigrama	programa
centigrama	espectrograma	radiograma
cladograma	estereograma	sismograma
criptograma	fanerógama	telegrama
cronograma	fonograma	
dendrograma	fotograma	
diagrama	hexagrama	

Spanish Shortcut

CHAPTER 28.
-EMA

Words ending in **EM** in English become **EMA** in Spanish.

Translate these words into Spanish and then check the answers on the next page.

1. ecosystem _____
2. emblem _____
3. phloem _____
4. photosystem _____
5. poem _____
6. problem _____
7. protoxylem _____
8. stratagem _____
9. subsystem _____
10. system _____
11. theorem _____

Spanish Shortcut

Here are the Spanish words. Check them. If you got them right, you will find many more words that you didn't know that you knew.

ecosistema	metaxilema	subsistema
emblema	poema	supersistema
estratagema	problema	teorema
exantema	floema	xilema
fotosistema	protoxilema	
gema	sistema	

Spanish Shortcut

CHAPTER 29.
-IO

Words ending in **UM** in English become **IO** in Spanish.

Translate these words into Spanish and then check the answers on the next page.

1. aluminium   _____
2. aquarium   _____
3. calcium   _____
4. magnesium   _____
5. podium   _____
6. potassium   _____
7. sodium   _____
8. stadium   _____
9. uranium   _____

Spanish Shortcut

Here are the Spanish words. Check them. If you got them right, you will find many more words that you didn't know that you knew.

actinio	exordio	plutonio
acuario	germanio	podio
alodio	helio	polonio
aluminio	hesperidio	potasio
americio	hidronio	presidio
amonio	himenio	primordio
armonio	hipantio	proscenio
atrio	holmio	prostomio
bario	ionio	protactinio
bedelio	iridio	radio
berilio	latifundio	renio
cadmio	litio	rodio
calcio	lutecio	rosario
californio	magnesio	rubidio
cerio	manubrio	rutenio
cesio	marsupio	sagrario
circonio	meconio	samario
colirio	mendelevio	sanatorio
columbio	mesotelio	selenio
compendio	micelio	sensorio
condominio	minio	silicio
crematorio	miracidio	simposio
cuadrivio	muonio	sincitio
curio	natatorio	sodio
decametonio	nefridio	estadio
deuterio	neptunio	talio
diazonio	niobio	tecnecio
diluvio	oceanario	terbio
disprosio	oidio	terrario
efluvio	opio	tetrazolio
endotecio	osmio	torio
endotelio	paladio	triclinio
equilibrio	peculio	triforio
erbio	peridio	tritio
escandio	perimisio	tulio
escritorio	pigidio	uranio

Spanish Shortcut

CHAPTER 30.
-URA

Words ending in **URE** in English become **URA** in Spanish.

Translate these words into Spanish and then check the answers on the next page.

1. adventure   _____
2. agriculture   _____
3. armature   _____
4. culture   _____
5. literature   _____
6. posture   _____
7. scripture   _____
8. sculpture   _____
9. tablature   _____
10. temperature _____
11. texture   _____
12. torture   _____

74

Spanish Shortcut

Here are the Spanish words. Check them. If you got them right, you will find many more words that you didn't know that you knew.

abertura	escultura	prefectura
acuicultura	estatura	prelatura
acupuntura	estructura	primogenitura
agricultura	fisura	púrpura
apicultura	flexura	ruptura
arboricultura	floricultura	sepultura
armadura	fractura	sericultura
arquitectura	genitura	silvicultura
aventura	horticultura	sinecura
avicultura	impostura	somatopleura
borradura	incisura	subcultura
candidatura	infraestructura	subliteratura
caricatura	investidura	subminiatura
censura	judicatura	superestructura
citricultura	legislatura	tablatura
comisura	ligadura	tecnoestructura
confitura	literatura	temperatura
conjetura	macroestructura	tesitura
contextura	magistratura	textura
contractura	maricultura	tintura
contracultura	microestructura	tonsura
coyuntura	microvasculatura	tortura
criatura	miniatura	ultimogenitura
cuadratura	musculatura	ultraestructura
cultura	nomenclatura	ultraminiatura
curvatura	nunciatura	ultrapura
dentadura	obertura	vasculatura
embocadura	piscicultura	vestidura
entabladura	postfractura	vinicultura
escritura	postura	viticultura

Spanish Shortcut

CHAPTER 31.
-TUD

Words ending in **TUDE** in English become **TUD** in Spanish.

Translate these words into Spanish and then check the answers on the next page.

1. altitude _____
2. amplitude _____
3. aptitude _____
4. gratitude _____
5. inaptitude _____
6. latitude _____
7. longitude _____
8. magnitude _____
9. multitude _____
10. plenitude _____
11. similitude _____
12. solicitude _____

Spanish Shortcut

Here are the Spanish words. Check them. If you got them right, you will find many more words that you didn't know that you knew.

altitud	ineptitud	negritud
amplitud	inexactitud	plenitud
aptitud	infinitud	prontitud
actitud	ingratitud	quietud
decrepitud	inquietud	rectitud
disimilitud	lasitud	similitud
exactitud	latitud	solicitud
finitud	longitud	vicisitud
gratitud	magnitud	
habitud	multitud	

Spanish Shortcut

CHAPTER 32.
-ADA

Words ending in **ADE** in English become **ADA** in Spanish.

Translate these words into Spanish and then check the answers on the next page.

1. arcade _____

2. barricade _____

3. brigade _____

4. cascade _____

5. charade _____

6. crusade _____

7. decade _____

8. facade _____

9. grenade _____

10. lemonade _____

Spanish Shortcut

Here are the Spanish words. Check them. If you got them right, you will find many more words that you didn't know that you knew.

alborada	cascada	galopada
alidada	charada	gasconada
arcada	cruzada	granada
arlequinada	década	limonada
balaustrada	digitígrada	mascarada
barricada	emboscada	mermelada
brigada	empalizada	pomada
cabalgada	fachada	retrógrada
carronada	fanfarronada	

Spanish Shortcut

CHAPTER 33.
-CIA

Words ending in **CY** in English become **CIA** in Spanish.

Translate these words into Spanish and then check the answers on the next page.

1. agency _____

2. aristocracy _____

3. bureaucracy _____

4. chiromancy _____

5. diplomacy _____

6. frequency _____

7. infancy _____

8. pharmacy _____

9. presidency _____

10. sufficiency _____

11. tendency _____

Spanish Shortcut

Here are the Spanish words. Check them. If you got them right, you will find many more words that you didn't know that you knew.

absorbencia	decencia	geomancia
agencia	deficiencia	gerontocracia
apetencia	delincuencia	ginecocracia
aristocracia	dependencia	hidromancia
astringencia	democracia	impotencia
autocracia	diplomacia	incipiencia
beligerancia	discordancia	inclemencia
burocracia	discrepancia	incompetencia
cadencia	divergencia	inconsecuencia
clemencia	eficacia	inconstancia
codependencia	eficiencia	incontinencia
coherencia	elegancia	inconveniencia
competencia	emergencia	incumbencia
complacencia	eminencia	indecencia
concurrencia	equivalencia	independencia
congruencia	estridencia	indiferencia
consistencia	excelencia	ineficacia
constancia	exigencia	infancia
contingencia	extravagancia	infrecuencia
contrainsurgencia	exuberancia	inmanencia
contumacia	falacia	inminencia
conveniencia	farmacia	inocencia
convergencia	flagrancia	insignificancia
corpulencia	flatulencia	insistencia
covalencia	fragancia	insolvencia
decadencia	frecuencia	insuficiencia

interdependencia
intermitencia
irrelevancia
lugartenencia
meritocracia
militancia
monocracia
nigromancia
emergencia
oclocracia
oniromancia
pendencia
permanencia
persistencia
pertinencia
petulancia
piromancia
potencia

precedencia
preeminencia
preponderancia
prepotencia
presidencia
prominencia
pudicicia
quiromancia
redundancia
regencia
repelencia
repugnancia
residencia
resistencia
sapiencia
solvencia
subyacencia
suficiencia

superintendencia
talasocracia
tangencia
tecnocracia
tendencia
tenencia
teocracia
timocracia
transparencia
trascendencia
turbulencia
turgencia
urgencia
vagancia
valencia
virulencia

Spanish Shortcut

CHAPTER 34. -FIA

Words ending in **PHY** in English become **FIA** in Spanish.

Translate these words into Spanish and then check the answers on the next page.

1. atrophy　　　　＿＿＿＿＿＿＿＿＿＿＿＿＿＿

2. autobiography　＿＿＿＿＿＿＿＿＿＿＿＿＿＿

3. autography　　＿＿＿＿＿＿＿＿＿＿＿＿＿＿

4. bibliography　　＿＿＿＿＿＿＿＿＿＿＿＿＿＿

5. calligraphy　　　＿＿＿＿＿＿＿＿＿＿＿＿＿＿

6. geography　　＿＿＿＿＿＿＿＿＿＿＿＿＿＿

7. orthography　　＿＿＿＿＿＿＿＿＿＿＿＿＿＿

8. photography　　＿＿＿＿＿＿＿＿＿＿＿＿＿＿

9. radiography　　＿＿＿＿＿＿＿＿＿＿＿＿＿＿

10. telegraphy　　＿＿＿＿＿＿＿＿＿＿＿＿＿＿

11. topography　　＿＿＿＿＿＿＿＿＿＿＿＿＿＿

Spanish Shortcut

Here are the Spanish words. Check them. If you got them right, you will find many more words that you didn't know that you knew.

angiografía	estereografía	oceanografía
antroposofía	estratigrafía	orografía
ortografía	etnografía	ortografía
arteriografía	eutrofia	oscilografía
astrofotografía	filmografía	paleogeografía
atrofia	filosofía	paleografía
autobiografía	fisiografía	petrografía
autografía	flebografía	pictografía
autorradiografía	flexografía	pletismografía
autotrofía	fluorografía	polarografía
bibliografía	fonocardiografía	pornografía
bioestratigrafía	fonografía	prosopografia
biogeografía	fotofluorografía	prototrofia
biografía	fotografía	psicobiografía
cacografía	fotolitografía	radioautografía
caligrafía	fotomicrografía	radiografía
cardiografía	fototelegrafía	radiotelegrafía
cartografia	gammagrafía	recromatografía
cinematografía	geografía	renografía
coreografía	hagiografía	reprografía
cosmografía	heterotrofia	serigrafía
criptografía	hidrografía	sismografía
cristalografía	hipertrofia	sofía
cromatografía	historiografía	telefotografía
cromolitografía	holografía	telegrafía
cronografía	iconografía	teosofía
demografía	ideografía	termografía
discografía	leucodistrofia	tipografía
distrofia	lexicografía	tomografía
ecografía	linfangiografía	topografía
electromiografía	linfografía	uranografía
encefalografía	litografía	venografía
endomorfia	macrofotografía	videografía
epigrafía	mamografía	xerografía
escenografía	metalografía	xilografía
espectrografía	microfotografía	zoogeografía
estenografía	microrradiografía	
estereofotografía	mitografía	

Spanish Shortcut

CHAPTER 35.
-ESO

Words ending in **ESS** in English become **ESO** in Spanish.

Translate these words into Spanish and then look up in a dictionary for the answers.

1. abscess   _____
2. access   _____
3. congress   _____
4. egress   _____
5. excess   _____
6. express   _____
7. gesso   _____
8. ingress   _____
9. process   _____
10. progress   _____

85

Spanish Shortcut

CHAPTER 36.
-OGO

Words ending in **GUE** in English become **OGO** in Spanish.

Translate these words into Spanish and then look up in a dictionary for the answers.

1. apologue   _____

2. catalog   _____

3. decalogue   _____

4. dialogue   _____

5. epilogue   _____

6. homologous   _____

7. logo   _____

8. monologue   _____

9. pedagogue   _____

CHAPTER 37.
-EA

Most English words that end in **EA** are exactly like the Spanish ones with a few small spelling changes.

Here are the Spanish words.

área	elodea	panacea
asea	espirea	piorrea
azalea	fóvea	polipnea
calcáneo	gonorrea	seborrea
corea	guinea	subárea
córnea	idea	tráquea
diarrea	miscelánea	tróclea
dismenorrea	náusea	urea
disnea	olea	úvea
dulcinea	palea	verborrea

Spanish Shortcut

CHAPTER 38.
-CULO

Words ending in **CLE** in English become **CULO** in Spanish.

Translate these words into Spanish and then check the answers on the next page.

1. article _____
2. circle _____
3. cycle _____
4. monocle _____
5. muscle _____
6. obstacle _____
7. oracle _____
8. tabernacle _____
9. testicle _____
10. tricycle _____
11. vehicle _____

88

Spanish Shortcut

Here are the Spanish words. Check them. If you got them right, you will find many more words that you didn't know that you knew.

antipartícula	funículo	periciclo
artículo	furúnculo	pináculo
cenáculo	hemiciclo	receptáculo
ciclo	heterociclo	retículo
círculo	kilociclo	semicírculo
conceptáculo	megaciclo	tabernáculo
corpúsculo	monociclo	tentáculo
cubículo	monóculo	testículo
dentículo	músculo	triciclo
epiciclo	obstáculo	tubérculo
espectáculo	oráculo	utrículo
espiráculo	pedículo	vehículo
fascículo	pedúnculo	
folículo	pentáculo	

Spanish Shortcut

CHAPTER 39.
-ANO

Words ending in **AN** in English become **ANO** in Spanish.

Translate these words into Spanish and then check the answers on the next page.

1. artisan _____
2. Castilian _____
3. Christian _____
4. human _____
5. Martian _____
6. ocean _____
7. organ _____
8. pagan _____
9. Presbyterian _____
10. Roman _____
11. vegetarian _____
12. vulcan _____

Spanish Shortcut

Here are the Spanish words. Check them. If you got them right, you will find many more words that you didn't know that you knew.

abeliano	furano	pretoriano
afgano	glucano	protohumano
antediluviano	huérfano	publicano
anticristiano	humano	puritano
antihumano	infrahumano	quitosano
araucano	inhumano	republicano
archidiocesano	interurbano	romano
artesano	manano	ruano
bosquimano	marciano	rurbano
castellano	mercaptano	samaritano
ceciliano	meridiano	sobrehumano
cipriano	metropolitano	suburbano
circadiano	miliciano	tímpano
ciudadano	océano	trépano
cordillerano	órgano	triptófano
cotidiano	otomano	urbano
cristiano	pagano	uretano
decano	paisano	vegetariano
decumano	parkinsoniano	veneciano
dextrano	parroquiano	veterano
diluviano	pelícano	vicedecano
diocesano	peptidoglicano	vulcano
dioxano	postdiluviano	
espartano	presbiteriano	

CHAPTER 40.
-IA

Most English words that end in **IA** are exactly like the Spanish ones with a few small spelling changes.

Here are the Spanish words.

abulia	anosmia	eulogia
acacia	anoxemia	eupepsia
academia	anoxia	eutanasia
acalasia	asfixia	fascia
acedia	astasia	feria
acequia	astenia	filaria
aclorhidria	asteria	fimbria
acolia	ataraxia	fobia
acondroplasia	ataxia	gloria
acrofobia	atresia	glosolalia
acromia	atrofia	hemofilia
actinia	bacteria	hemoglobinuria
adularia	begonia	hernia
adventicia	bohemia	hidrofobia
aerobia	Bolivia	hipercapnia
agenesia	difteria	hiperemia
agnosia	diluvia	hiperfagia
agorafobia	disfagia	hiperglucemia
albuminuria	disfasia	hiperlipemia
alexia	dislexia	hipermedia
amnesia	dispepsia	hipermnesia
analgesia	eclampsia	hiperplasia
anemia	ecolalia	hiperquinesia
anergia	ectopia	hipertermia
anestesia	enciclopedia	homofobia
angaria	estancia	
anorexia	euforia	

Spanish Shortcut

CHAPTER 41.
-PLO or -PLIO

Words ending in **PLE** in English become **PLO** or **PLIO** in Spanish.

Translate these words into Spanish and then look up in a dictionary for the answers.

1. ample _____

2. centuple _____

3. example _____

4. principle _____

5. quadruple _____

6. scruple _____

7. sextuple _____

8. submultiple _____

9. temple _____

Spanish Shortcut

CHAPTER 42. -INA

Words ending in **IN or INE** in English become **INA or INO** in Spanish.

Translate these words into Spanish and then check the answers on the next page.

1. adrenalin _____
2. amoxicillin _____
3. amphetamine _____
4. antitoxin _____
5. aspirin _____
6. assassin _____
7. Bedouin _____
8. bobbin _____
9. caffeine _____
10. penguin _____
11. vitamin _____

Spanish Shortcut

Here are the Spanish words. Check them. If you got them right, you will find many more words that you didn't know that you knew.

acetina	amoxicilina	auxina
aciloína	ampicilina	avidina
acroleína	anatoxina	azatioprina
actina	anfetamina	azidotimidina
adenosina	angiotensina	azina
adrenalina	anilina	bacitracina
aecuorina	antiglobulina	bacterina
aeromedicina	antimicina	bacteriocina
aglutinina	antipirina	beduino
aguamarina	antitoxina	beguina
alanina	antitrombina	bilirrubina
alantoína	antivitamina	biotina
albúmina	antocianina	bobina
alizarina	apomorfina	cabina
almandina	arecolina	cafeína
aloína	argentina	calcitonina
amanitina	arginina	calicreína
amantadina	arsfenamina	calidina
amidina	arsina	cretino
amigdalina	asesino	lupino
amilopectina	asparagina	pingüino
amina	aspirina	platino
aminofilina	atrazina	rabino
aminopirina	atropina	vitamina

Spanish Shortcut

CHAPTER 43.
-ENO

Words ending in **EN** in English become **ENO** in Spanish.

Translate these words into Spanish and then check the answers on the next page.

1. anticancerigene _____

2. antigen _____

3. estrogen _____

4. glycogen _____

5. halogen _____

6. hydrogen _____

7. kerogen _____

8. nitrogen _____

9. oxygen _____

10. pathogen _____

Spanish Shortcut

Here are the Spanish words. Check them. If you got them right, you will find many more words that you didn't know that you knew.

aglutinógeno	criógeno	nitrógeno
alérgeno	endógeno	oxígeno
aloantígeno	estrógeno	patógeno
alucinógeno	felógeno	pepsinógeno
anticancerígeno	fibrinógeno	plasminógeno
antiestrógeno	fitopatógeno	progestágeno
antígeno	glucógeno	tripsinógeno
calcógeno	halógeno	tropocolágeno
carcinógeno	hidrógeno	zimógeno
cianogeno	inmunógeno	
colágeno	kerógeno	

CHAPTER 44.
-AR Words

Most English words that end in **AR** are exactly like the Spanish ones with a few small spelling changes.

Here are the Spanish words.

acelular	biomolecular	espectacular
acetabular	bipolar	extracelular
acicular	bolívar	extraescolar
altar	bulbar	extravascular
angular	canicular	familiar
antinuclear	capsular	fibrilar
antipopular	cardiovascular	foliar
antisolar	caviar	funicular
anular	celular	gastrovascular
apendicular	cerebrovascular	glandular
arteriolar	circular	globular
articular	circumpolar	impopular
avascular	circunestelar	interestelar
avatar	consular	intermolecular
avicular	corpuscular	irregular
axilar	cuadrangular	jacamar
bacillar	cupular	jaguar
bar	curricular	lunar
basilar	cuticular	minibar
bazar	dólar	modular
bimolecular	ejemplar	molecular
binocular	escalar	mononuclear

Spanish Shortcut

multicar	popular	trilinear
multicelular	premolar	trinocular
multipolar	radar	tubular
muscular	radicular	ungular
néctar	rectangular	unicelular
nodular	regular	unifilar
nuclear	semilunar	uvular
ocular	similar	vacuolar
opercular	singular	valvular
particular	solar	vascular
peculiar	tabular	ventricular
perpendicular	testicular	vestibular
pilar	transpolar	yugular
polar	triangular	

Spanish Shortcut

CHAPTER 45.
-METRO/-RO

Words ending in **ER** in English become **RO** in Spanish.

Translate these words into Spanish and then check the answers on the next page.

1. accelerometer _____
2. centimeter _____
3. chronometer _____
4. decameter _____
5. decimeter _____
6. diameter _____
7. hydrometer _____
8. kilometer _____
9. meter _____
10. millimeter _____
11. perimeter _____
12. taximeter _____

Spanish Shortcut

Here are the Spanish words. Check them. If you got them right, you will find many more words that you didn't know that you knew.

acelerómetro	densitómetro	galvanómetro
actinómetro	diámetro	gasómetro
aerómetro	difractómetro	goniómetro
altímetro	dilatómetro	gradiómetro
amperímetro	dinamómetro	gravímetro
anemómetro	dosímetro	hectolitro
atmómetro	durómetro	hectómetro
audiómetro	electrómetro	heliómetro
barómetro	ergómetro	hemocitómetro
bolómetro	escintilómetro	hidrómetro
calorímetro	esclerómetro	higrómetro
ceilómetro	esferómetro	hipocentro
centímetro	espectrómetro	kilómetro
cetro	espirómetro	magnetómetro
clinómetro	eudiómetro	manómetro
colorímetro	extensómetro	metro
coulómetro	fluorímetro	micrómetro
cronómetro	fluorómetro	milímetro
decámetro	fotómetro	olfatómetro
decímetro	fotopolarímetro	osmómetro

parámetro
perímetro
períptero
planímetro
podómetro
polarímetro
psicrómetro
radiómetro
reflectómetro
refractómetro
sacarímetro
salinómetro

semidiámetro
sensitómetro
subministro
superministro
tacómetro
taxímetro
telémetro
telurómetro
tenderómetro
tensiómetro
termómetro
tetrámetro

tonómetro
urinómetro
variómetro
vatímetro
velocímetro
viscosímetro
voltímetro
volúmetro

CHAPTER 46.
-OR

Most English words that end in **OR** are exactly like the Spanish ones with a few small spelling changes.

Here are the Spanish words.

asesor	corruptor	furor
auditor	cursor	genitor
autor	depresor	Héctor
actor	descriptor	horror
benefactor	detector	humor
bicolor	detractor	impostor
biosensor	difusor	impulsor
castor	digestor	inceptor
clamor	director	inductor
coadjutor	disector	inferior
coautor	divisor	inspector
codirector	doctor	institutor
coeditor	dolor	instructor
cofactor	editor	intercesor
coinventor	efector	interdictor
color	elector	interior
compositor	erector	interlocutor
compresor	error	interruptor
conductor	estupor	interventor
conector	expositor	inventor
confesor	extensor	inversor
confiteor	exterior	inyector
constrictor	extractor	licor
constructor	eyector	locomotor
consultor	factor	menor
contradictor	fervor	multicolor
convector	flexor	multiplexor
corrector	flúor	objetor

obstructor
pastor
posterior
preceptor
precursor
predecesor
pretor
previsor
profesor
progenitor
prolocutor
propretor
prosector
protector
proyector
raptor
reactor
receptor
reconstructor
rector
redactor

reductor
reflector
refractor
relator
represor
resistor
revisor
semiconductor
signor
subdirector
subsector
sucesor
superconductor
superior
supervisor
supresor
tabor
temblor
tenor
tensor
termistor

terror
torpor
tractor
traductor
transgresor
transistor
tricolor
trimotor
trisector
tumor
tutor
ulterior
unicolor
valor
vapor
varactor
vector
viator
vigor

Spanish Shortcut

CHAPTER 47.
VERB SHORTCUT

This chapter will help you to learn more verb shortcuts. It will help you further in your pursuit to fluency in Spanish.

Translate these verbs into English.

abogar   _____

acelerar   _____

aceptar   _____

acezar   _____

acreditar   _____

actuar   _____

acusar   _____

adaptar   _____

adoptar   _____

adornar   _____

afirmar   _____

ajustar   _____

alarmar   _____

alertar   _____

alterar   _____

anestesiar   _____

Spanish Shortcut

curvar _____

decidir _____

declarar _____

definir _____

defraudar _____

depositar _____

detallar _____

detectar _____

detestar _____

diagnosticar _____

diagramar _____

disertar _____

distanciar _____

distribuir _____

dividir _____

divorciar _____

documentar _____

drogar _____

eclipsar _____

editar _____

ejecutar _____

ejercitar _____

eletrocultar _____

Spanish Shortcut

elevar _____

enmascarar _____

entusiasmar _____

equipar _____

escanear _____

escapar _____

esquiar _____

estructurar _____

evidenciar _____

exclamar _____

expandir _____

experimentar _____

extractar _____

fantasiar _____

fermentar _____

fijar _____

filmar _____

flexionar _____

florar _____

formentar _____

florestar _____

formar _____

formular _____

Spanish Shortcut

fotografiar　　　＿＿＿＿＿＿＿＿＿＿

fracionar　　　　＿＿＿＿＿＿＿＿＿＿

frasear　　　　　＿＿＿＿＿＿＿＿＿＿

funcionar　　　　＿＿＿＿＿＿＿＿＿＿

galopar　　　　　＿＿＿＿＿＿＿＿＿＿

guiar　　　　　　＿＿＿＿＿＿＿＿＿＿

igualar　　　　　＿＿＿＿＿＿＿＿＿＿

impedir　　　　　＿＿＿＿＿＿＿＿＿＿

importar　　　　＿＿＿＿＿＿＿＿＿＿

impresionar　　　＿＿＿＿＿＿＿＿＿＿

inalar　　　　　　＿＿＿＿＿＿＿＿＿＿

indexar　　　　　＿＿＿＿＿＿＿＿＿＿

infectar　　　　　＿＿＿＿＿＿＿＿＿＿

inmigar　　　　　＿＿＿＿＿＿＿＿＿＿

inspeccionar　　　＿＿＿＿＿＿＿＿＿＿

instruir　　　　　＿＿＿＿＿＿＿＿＿＿

instrumentar　　　＿＿＿＿＿＿＿＿＿＿

interferir　　　　＿＿＿＿＿＿＿＿＿＿

interpretar　　　　＿＿＿＿＿＿＿＿＿＿

laborar　　　　　＿＿＿＿＿＿＿＿＿＿

licenciar　　　　　＿＿＿＿＿＿＿＿＿＿

limitar　　　　　＿＿＿＿＿＿＿＿＿＿

mapear　　　　　＿＿＿＿＿＿＿＿＿＿

Spanish Shortcut

marcar _____

medicinar _____

microfilmar _____

migrar _____

modelar _____

multiplicar _____

navegar _____

nominar _____

notar _____

nutrir _____

oprimir _____

optar _____

orientar _____

partir _____

pasar _____

pedalear _____

perdonar _____

perfumar _____

permanecer _____

perseverar _____

persistir _____

pervertir _____

pilotar _____

Spanish Shortcut

pintar _____

planear _____

plantar _____

ponderar _____

practicar _____

prescribir _____

probar _____

procesar _____

profesar _____

programar _____

prolongar _____

prometer _____

prostituir _____

protestar _____

proyectar _____

puntuar _____

radiografiar _____

recepcionar _____

refrigerar _____

registrar _____

regresar _____

reportar _____

represar _____

Spanish Shortcut

reservar _____

residir _____

resolver _____

respectar _____

responder _____

retribuir _____

reunir _____

revelar _____

revertir _____

rodar _____

rodear _____

rosar _____

salvar _____

seducir _____

segmentar _____

seleccionar _____

sentenciar _____

sostener _____

suceder _____

sumar _____

tasar _____

telefonear _____

terminar _____

traficar _____

titular _____

transformar _____

transgredir _____

transportar _____

triunfar _____

ventilar _____

violar _____

vomitar _____

votar _____

Talk to the Author
Email: irineu@oliveiralanguageservices.com

Printed in Great Britain
by Amazon